Inner SANCTUARY

Inner SANCTUARY

LIFETIME MUSINGS OF A POET

Robert E. Shaffer

INNER SANCTUARY
LIFETIME MUSINGS OF A POET

iUniverse books may be ordered through booksellers or by contacting:

iUniverse
1663 Liberty Drive
Bloomington, IN 47403
www.iuniverse.com
1-800-Authors (1-800-288-4677)

Because of the dynamic nature of the Internet, any web addresses or links contained in this book may have changed since publication and may no longer be valid. The views expressed in this work are solely those of the author and do not necessarily reflect the views of the publisher, and the publisher hereby disclaims any responsibility for them.

Any people depicted in stock imagery provided by Thinkstock are models, and such images are being used for illustrative purposes only. Certain stock imagery © Thinkstock.

ISBN: 978-1-4917-8272-9 (sc)
ISBN: 978-1-4917-8273-6 (e)

Library of Congress Control Number: 2015918353

Print information available on the last page.

iUniverse rev. date: 11/18/2015

Contents

Dedication

This book is dedicated to the Ellsworth High School English Literature teachers who were my inspirations: Mabel Herzog, Phyllis Francis and A.L. Farrington. To my mother Leola Shaffer, who raised two boys on her own and made a career of teaching. To my longtime close friend and mentor, Ben D. Mahaffey. Finally, to my spouse, Tina, my special angel, who not only supported me in making my life's dream happen, but also spent hours typing my manuscript.

Foreword

Years ago, Bob showed me some of his poetry. I always enjoyed reading his various works. He has the talent and wording to make his stanzas come alive; sometimes they seem to actually reach out and grab me. At other times, I have to stop, think, and let his words sink into my conscious being.

Prose can inform, move, and motivate people. But poetry can create a sense of passion! You will realize this as you read Bob's book. I am pleased to recommend this, his first contribution to the great body of poetic works.

Ben D. Mahaffey
St. George, Utah

My Sanctuary

I Wonder What Tomorrow Will Bring

I wonder what tomorrow
    will bring.
I just hope tomorrow comes
    bright and fair.
I'm tired of these dismal
gray days today.
And I think
    I felt the same yesterday
        as I feel today.
Yesterday's tomorrow was today.
But no change is there.
I hear that each man
    is the master of his own destiny.
This must be so.
But I don't change.
I look for a brighter tomorrow
    but fail to see the light today.
Are there others like me?
If I could only see today's light
    I might find a brighter tomorrow.

Autumn Reflection

What magic children bring.
To see them we wonder.
Can they be a part of us,
   coming through us,
   although they pass
     beyond our grasp?
The poets are right.
We cannot go to them and
   they cannot come to us.
We are separated parts,
unable to become one.
And, yet,
   children cannot be
   separated from adults,
     nor can adults be
     separated from children.
Children weave magic in their being.
To know that they come from us,
   a hope and promise of
     future greatness springs.
And we were once children, ourselves.
We were once magical children.
Have we forgotten?

Today

Harsh times.
Bleak times.
Cruel times.
Times of despair.
Times of greed.
Times of hope.
Today.

Thoughts seem dry,
and words become twisted.
Life without success
isn't really life.
There is no living
without fulfillment.
All to say we must forget ...
   today.

But,
like yesterday,
we remain.
Desperately groping
for impossible dreams.
There is no forgetting.
Just living ...
   today.

A Blind Man

A man can sometimes
be so ignorant he just cannot see.
This is often true
when he deals with other men.
Prejudice is born out of
misunderstanding.
Hatred out of fear.
A man's destiny
Is forged by these things.
Ideals come and go
as the passing of a summer breeze;
all because,
being a blind man
with his foolish ways,
they have no grounds
for permanence.

Often I feel there is a chance
for a blind man.
There must be.
Hatred cannot continue forever.
But, then I resign

myself to apparent facts.
There will be no change,
there can never be change.
My hopes stem from dreams,
The dreams are uprooted,
and I can do nothing,
for I too am a blind man.

Let us Rejoice

Let us rejoice and be exceeding glad,
for I have found my drunken dad
in a pool hall
leaning against a wall.
He was not a bad man, although
he brought my mother much woe.
His intentions were good, however,
his drinking made him say never
to all of his plans,
to all of his plans.

Misinterpretations

I remember those days well.
Misinterpretations -- little else.
A false autumn with red, yellow and brown
leaves lying on the ground and blowing
helter-skelter in the crisp wind.
A chill in the air meant nothing:
all was gone. Dead.
The dry, brown grass blanketed the earth
and brought remembrances.
It was finished. Life was dead.
I remember those days well.

Doom Flood

That was the flood; an influx
Of fools on an average society.
American, Russians. Hating
One another because someone lied.
Truth equals falsehood.
The world's greatest powers lost
In the chaos of propaganda –
Hoping vainly to win world domination.
And all because a few lied.
Fools perish: we are doomed.

Argument Against Divorce

I walk down the street
with the wind blowing in my face,
and I think of you.
You mean more to me than
I can say. I worship you.

I know it's silly,
but you are my woman.
You're the only girl I
could possibly care about,
and more.

We were made for each other.
Can't you see that, my love?
We argue, we cry, but still we belong
together. We should not be separated.
And you don't understand.
Do you?

I Am

While growing up I yearned
    and longed for adulthood.
As an adult I grieve for
my lost childhood.

My life is a tapestry of
  color and shadow, laughter
    and grief, pain and
     rapture.

Much of my youth was spent
in the fifties – such a gentle time.
    And yet, it was a time
of agony and despair.
    At least for me.

But I see it all in quiet memory.
    My family was whole and
     complete.
Now they are all gone.
    I mourn.

My childhood fears and uncertainties
    have been replaced by adult
        recollections.
What was black is now
a hazy shade of gray;
    not threatening.
Who am I?
    I am.

Moon Child

Child of the moon,
  lonely,
    moody,
      pensive,
aware only of the
  war within his soul,
gropes desperately
  for the peace and hope
    which are not there.
Laughter and contentment,
  things to be desired
    and had by most,
evade the melancholy
  child of the moon;
the child which is
  the father of man,
  of man the father.
    Ourselves.

Broken Promises

Broken promises are all
   that can be,
shattered dreams that
   can't come true.
Such is life in a world
of mere existence.
Friends seem enemies,
enemies seem friends, allies.
Why?
Where is the old good?
Lost in the whirlwind of time.
Winds of change have come
and a shadow moves
   across the land.
Nowhere is authority to be trusted.
Lives are spent, lies spoken.
This is the agony of
promises broken.
Someday men may dwell
   in truth and peace.
Until that near or distant time,
promises remain – broken.

Landscape with Running Figures

Life is full of shadows,
a landscape with running figures.
Events come and go
like the passing of a breeze
which incessantly
rustles the leaves and grass,
only to pass, and not return.

Thoughts return
as if to grasp what was once
today, reality.
But the fleeting fingers
of memory are greased
with haze.

Enough cannot be remembered;
it never will.

Scenes fly past.
Only haze remains.
Mists of dawn cover a
landscape with running figures.

Tomorrow will come
and become yesterday.
Nothing ever stays the same.

And ...
enough cannot be remembered.
It never will.

Nemesis

What manner of creature
   are you who come
     to bring sorrow and pain?
Away, Nemesis, away!
There is little need of
   your presence
     here today.
You work with diligence
and bring disaster and despair.
We have had quite enough
   of you lately, Nemesis,
so be gone, away!
But alas, you ever remain
   to torment and torture
     the spirit, the mind.
Take your greed and lust
   elsewhere, now.
Get thee hence!

The End Is but the Beginning

It grows, it ripens,
    it's harvested, it dies.
Such is the cycle of life.
Wheat, grain, crops,
Each in turn feels life
    and then death.
So it is with all that grows.
An end must always come.

People all too often desire
    death to pass them by.
They must be cowards
to feel fear of death so.
If all things must die,
then people, too, must cease.
But in dying they live on,
at least that part we
call spirit, soul.

Therefore, immortality is real.
We must simply fall asleep
    to achieve the dream.

An end must always come.
So it is with all that grows.

    But ...
        the end is but the beginning.

Subtle Thing

Loneliness is a subtle thing.
It lurks within each heart
    and is only felt on occasion.
When this spell –
    and that's what it is –
hits, we feel empty,
almost lost, and sad.
Sadness is often born of
    loneliness;
loneliness born of fatigue.
If fatigue were the only answer
    then we need not feel
    the sting or lash of
        loneliness.

But loneliness hits when we
are even rested and alert.
Our loneliness must arise
    from something within
    our inner selves.
Not that it matters gravely,
for underneath is the subtle thing.

All have it, even the person
    amid great company.
Loneliness is, therefore, the
    desire, the wish to
find companionship in other
    than people.
Maybe not a subtle thing – loneliness –
but a fact of life.

Walking

Walking seems to be the solution
when an individual has a problem
he wants to work out.
Walking gives a person
the time to think about and solve his problem.
Walking ...
   Walking ...
      Walking ...

I have not found a better solution.
How about you?

Scapegoat

Behold the scapegoat,
   the King.
He dies and accepts
   the punishment
     for others.
And not a marvel is He
but a man doing His duty,
giving His all for His brothers.
Someday a page in history
   will be written giving
the scapegoat honor and praise
   for a cause most just.
It is only we, those living
in the present, who do not
   appreciate or believe.
Pity us, the living, who
behold the scapegoat,
   the King,
and turn asunder.

If I Can But Do Good in Life

If I can but do good in life
   perhaps my existence will have
   meant something when I am
     no more.
I cannot conceive of hearing
   a child cry and not shed
   a tear.
I behold the homeless and hopeless
   and willingly hold out my hand.
I meet the abusers and users
and desire to counsel and admonish.
   And all those who are full of
   hate and destruction and have
     eyes burning with lust
     and greed and corrupt
     desire, I forgive.

If I can but do good in life
   then I can build a chain,
   a link of souls who carry on
the look of love and compassion,
and present a wellspring of charity
   and kindness which may
   mushroom into a pillar of safety
   and joy and peace.

Yes, and yes.
    If I can but do good in life
perhaps others may gain such
       a desire and join in the dream.
    And share the testimony of
good news and cheer.
     Then, oh then, all
    is not lost and ever
     so meaningless.

If I can but do good in life.

To A Friend

I need a friend.
Though you say it's not you
I need, I do.
It's strange the way
things have a habit of happening.
And friendships come and go,
maybe like ours.
Still, I need a friend like you.
   Only you …
      friend.

Rockies I

The mountains live in my memory,
    their majesty and grandeur
    are the essence of all
that is real and wonderful.
I behold the snowcapped peaks,
    the rugged tree-line,
    the flower studded meadows,
and I sing with joy. My heart
swells with wondrous exaltation.

These are the mountains,
    a world of rugged beauty.
Here only peace swells, in the
silence of nature, that cannot
    be forgotten when in
    town or city, or on the plains.
Nothing can compare to the sound
of the bubbling brook and
    the rustle of the aspens in a
    the breeze, as nature passes by.

I cannot forget my love for these
   rugged sentinels and my
   longing to return to them.
They are always before me in
   my quiet thoughts, and hopes,
   and schemes.
Thus, the majestic Rockies.
   Pinnacles that live in my soul
   as I dwell in their shadow.

A Measure of Dust

People are looked at by
a measure of dust.
People don't stop to think of
    what is to be or may have been.
People seem at a loss
as to the thread of life.
No measure is meted out
    other than thoughts of the end.
And in the end people look
    at themselves as but a measure.
        A measure if dust.

Journey

The distant shores wait.
　　Their call beckons as if
through a distant mist,
and I heed their call.

I wander through shady
　　landscapes of wonder and
unseemly mystery, majesty.
And on the gentle breezes
　　voices whisper secrets of old.
I hear them call out to me – -
　　come, come and behold.

I traverse far on the narrow
　　crooked pathways of destiny,
overcoming all the pitfalls and
treacherous landslides I come
　　to find and to know.

And on this journey through
　　shades of darkness and
　　disquieting foggy mists,

I perceive the light.
    The road is found
  to that far-off shore - -
    that distant land - -
      paradise.

Life Magic

Where is the magic?
Oh, where has it gone?
   Years pass and nothing
   seems to remain of
     the bright youthful
      innocence.

Can it be that I have changed
   all that much over
   the years?
     And who is that
   stranger I behold in the mirror?
Surely that unknown is not
   who I am.
     But is that shape
     I perceive who I
      once was?

Tomorrow may come with all
   her changes and hopes
   and dreams.
      And there is the dream time;
   a connection with the inner child.

The magic is still there.
   I am who I am -
      and was.

Thoughts

Why must a man be chained
   body and soul?
Why can't he be free?
Just because that man
   is black
      should never dictate
         otherwise.
All are equal in God's sight.
There is great injustice
   in the world.
Man killing man,
   violent torture,
      denial of human
   dignity and rights.

I hope for a day when all mankind
   will be equal,
      free and proud,
   living as brothers.
But first we must learn.
   We must share and
      care together.
We must forgive and trust.
Let the killing and hatred stop.

   I am my brothers' keeper.

South Africa '77

I wake and hear crying
    and screams,
and the dreadful sound
    of gunfire
        in the night.
I behold, and cry.
    That lifeless body
        was once a child.
    What was his crime?
Where's the justice in
    his murder?
For me the screams
    of this tragedy
        never end.
    I close my eyes to sleep
        and I see
            rivers of blood.
I cannot close my ears
    to the cries,
        the groans,
    of those yearning
        to breathe free.

Oh, God, where
    is justice,
        brotherhood?

Dream Time

This is the dream time.
Reality hidden by shadows.
   Tomorrow is but a distant
      shore, shrouded in mist,
      bleak, bare.
Yesterday is only a vast
   chasm, unreachable, lost,
      so very forlorn.

All that remains is
the dream time,
   veiled with mystery, magic;
      a wizard's spell
      conjured from the
   deepest, darkest recesses
      of the mind, bridged
      only by the strongest fantasy.

Yes.
   This is the dream time.
   Darkness becoming reality.
      Reality becoming light.
      A true awakening.

Always

I see and hear you in my dreams.
   You are always there at my
   side to counsel and comfort.

But upon waking I know you
   are gone, passed on to the
   other sphere of existence.
     You are lost to me.
   You who I have known all
     my days.

So strange, so odd.

I cannot imagine someone
   whom I have loved is no more.
   It just cannot be.
     You must be there.

All is lost.
   It must be a truth
   that love remains,
     if only in memory,
   and the deep longing of
   my heart.

You are there,
   always, always.

Mystery

Do you love the stars?
Can you feel their presence
and hear them call your name?

    An unusual thought.

But to dream is envious
and that's the way to stars.
Darkness is broken
    by radiant light,
shattered almost,
    to be presumed
dead until tomorrow night.

    A strange thought.

Words

Words.
Nothing much.
Small talk.
   Unimportant sounds.
Words put together make phrases.
The phrases become sentences,
   paragraphs.
And with paragraphs
   come the poems, plays,
   stories, and novels.
Words are simple until used;
used to express ideas.
That's all we have –
small talk, dreams,
   loose words.
No one listens to the plans
idealized in thoughts.
We just go on and pray.
And what of prayer?
Words.
   Nothing much.
      Small talk.
         Unimportant sounds?

The Old Elm

It stands now only in my memory.
   A great old elm -- sentinel
   at my grandparents
      front parking—
   tall and spread out.

I see the little boy
   standing beneath the
      stately boughs
      and marveling
   at its rich enchantment.

That boy would gaze
   at the great majesty
      and listen to secrets
      told as the wind passed
   through that green leafy tapestry.

The tales told were those
   common to the human child.
      A portent of things
      yet to come to pass
   and a history of all that has been.

I behold that marvelous old elm,
  and the boy beneath its arms,
    cradled in such cool
    shade and quiet solitude;
  and perceive – I am that boy.

Oh, to have you, my beloved
  great and grand old elm,
    stand sentinel once again
    at the rapture of childhood
  and the dawn of this my life.

On Looking Back at the Past

Looking back at the past
is a subject of much controversy.
We all look back at the past
in some manner or the other.
Many cherish past moments,
some long to relive what is no more.
The past ...
We too often dwell on that which we should let go.
Never regret your loss, however,
for much will be gained as replacement in the future.
And fear not the future,
since tomorrow takes care of itself,
and time, blessed time, heals all wounds.

I Cannot See Clearly

I cannot see clearly.
Everywhere I look I
    behold shades of gray.
All is melancholy, shrouded,
    shadowed by time.
Everything is as a mist
    growing deeper, thicker.
Pain is in the beginning
    never ending,
        always perceived.

Life is viewed as in
    a cracked looking glass,
        forlorn and bleak.
Colors dark and unmovable,
    grow only dimmer with
        the passing of time.

Thus is evil spread around
    and abroad.
Youth is fleeting, a memory
    gone and fading into
        obscurity.
Lost!
    All is lost,
    nothing gained.

Tomorrow May Come

Tomorrow may come in splendor
  and triumph, shouting
  for recognition and
    understanding.
And tomorrow may fade
  into obscurity and oh so
  bleak desolation,
    crying for pity and relief.
Next week, next month, next year,
  come and bring what
    may be
  echoed in the halls
  of eternity, an endless time
    of joy and regrets.
And all to the eyes of
the beholder.
Tomorrow may come, and come,
  and then disappear.
    Tomorrow, tomorrow.

Her Face

Her face.
That's what caught my eye.

Some may have thought her face
    to be ordinary;
just another face in the crowd
    of life.
Yes, a face which represented
nothing but a nameless number.

So they thought.
    So let them think still.

I knew more than they.
I saw more than they,
    much more, in her face.
Her face.
That's what caught my eye.

When I first beheld that face
I was compelled to stare.
Love, joy, peace, and more
    were written thereon;
written in the hair of gold,
the eyes of blue, and the smile – -

the smile of an angel.

That face belonged to someone,
 someone who would be remembered.
My joy was in beholding
 such beauty.

Her face.

Because You Are My Friend

Because you are my friend,
my heart
is always open.
  There is nothing I hold back
  and nothing not freely given.
I am here to listen to your hopes
and dreams and flights of fantasy.
  My shoulder is broad enough
  to comfort and console when sad.
Your secrets will be mine.
In my caring you can trust.
  Yes, I will always prove faithful.
  All this because you are my friend.

Far Away

I reach for the sun
and I walk on the moon.
   My life is an endless journey
   paving my way to destiny.
I glimpse the stars and I
marvel at each unique pillar of light.
   The dream quest I began at birth
   is more than half accomplished.
My destination as humble traveler is
glimpsed only rarely, if at all.
   Eternity is my ultimate planted seed
   based in love and hope and faith.
And so I reach longingly for the sun
perchance to walk among the valleys of the moon
   reunited with my relative traveler seekers.
   who blazed the trail to lands oh so far away.

Mystique

I saw her.
That girl, woman, of my dreams.
Was she a shadow
    from the past,
or a glimpse of the future?
        I could not say.
I only knew I had found
    someone special.

Was she a dream,
    a whim,
        a false hope?
    Never! Never!

She was real enough.
And it seemed so odd
    that someone so loving,
        so very beautiful,
    should show the least
interest in me.
I must have done something
    good sometime
        to deserve one
            oh, so unique.

And what about our tomorrows?
 I could not, cannot say.
  Only One knows
 what will be.

And there lies my desire.
 And there lies my hope.
  My love.

Life

Sometime back I stumbled.
I got right up and grumbled.
"It just isn't fair," said I
When I noticed my black eye.
This just shouldn't be.
It's a curse aimed just at me.
But, alas, it is my plot
To never shun my lot
Of life and future plan.
After all, I'm just a man.

The Quiet Place

I took a walk to the quiet place
    just to spend some time and think.
My revelations were not great;
    they would never inspire nations,
        nor would they move mountains,
    but they suited my needs
        and became inspiration.

Night

The night creeps round us like a movie monster.
It dwells with us in our fears and quiet thoughts
and offers only mystery.
Such is the night;
a shadow which disappears gradually
clinging to life.

Rain

Rain is so refreshing!
It gently falls
   bringing drink
to thirsty Mother Earth.

I Wonder Why

I wonder why we should fear
for all those things held dear.
We cannot take them with us
so why all the fuss?
Our riches come from actions
which bring about true reactions
from those whose lives we share,
the brothers for whom we care.
Love was put in our hearts not to keep
but to give away lest we should weep.
Because of this great thought
and all it has brought
I say to you, my friend,
from now until the very end,
I shall always be here.
I shall always be near.

A Dream of Trucking

When I was young
I heard the call of the diesel
　　by day and night
and watched the trucks
　　as they roared by.

Trucking seemed the life to lead.
Being able to move from place to place
　　and seeing parts of the country
few chanced to see in their lifetime
　　would be grand.

And the adventure of it all
　　would surely be great.
Why, a trucker becomes part
　　of every city and town
he chances to touch with
　　his life.
There's Chicago, Omaha, Seattle,
　　Frisco, L. A., Cleveland,
　　Montgomery, Dallas, Atlanta,
　　El Paso, Portland, Cheyenne,
　　　and hundreds more.
And all beckoning.

Such is the life of the trucker;
　　the lifeblood, the backbone of the nation.

Rockies II

I behold the craggy, snow-capped
  granite peaks with awe.
Only above the timberline
  do the majestic spires lift
  up their heads toward heaven.
The Rockies, the sphere of
  gurgling streams and frosty
    mountain lakes.
Meadows of wild flowers and grasses
  blowing in the gentle, pure
    mountain breezes, dot
    the landscape among
  the firs and pines and aspen.

This is the high country,
  a realm of wonder and
    such stark beauty.
Clouds float gently overhead,
  and eagles and hawks soar.
Deer and elk and wondrous
  wildlife roam in the bastion
    of nature's spectacle.
Nowhere else is there such
  diverse grandeur.

Thus we have the Rockies,
    a diverse, unique mountain range.
Each peak, each valley, each pass
    has its own story.
Here is where the Indian dwelt
    and roamed with peace
        and security.
Here is where the trapper -- the
    mountain man -- made
        his living and had
        a robust lust
            for life.

The Rockies, my love,
    my life, my home.

Travel by Bus

Travel by bus.
Can there be a greater nightmare?
It seems such a painful --
   and oh so drawn out --
      journey.
Each bump and crack in
   the road tries to send
      you to the moon.
And the jolting and swaying
   of the bus will certainly
      rearrange your innards.

Travel by bus.
Can anything bring more peril?
Every twenty miles or so
   there is that unavoidable
      road construction!
How dreadful are the signs
   which read – one way traffic
      next forty miles.
Oh the pain, the pain.

Travel by bus.
Can anything be more boring?
Every five miles there

appears another little town.
and the driver says, "We will now
    take a half hour rest stop."
Such a bore!

Next summer when I take
    my annual trip,
I think I shall travel --
    by bus!

    This trip was fun!

I was Young Once

I was young once.
    It seems like such a distant past,
when all was innocence.
        No cares.

Things seem to fade with time.
    Old acquaintances slip into memory.
Time marches on and the fleeting
        moment dies.

I was young once
    So green, so gold.
Now all is tarnished and brown.
      the day fades.
    Evening has come.
    The sun goes down on life.

    Yes,
        I was young once.

Oh, to be so free.

Salvation

Lost
silent
damned
man.

Hollow
stuffed
spineless
man.

Sad
melancholy
pensive
man.

Life
light
peace
Jesus.

Love
hope
joy
God.

The Prophet

When first I saw him
I was a young man.
He spoke of truth and life,
love and knowledge,
and faith as strong
   as life itself.
And I wondered.

Next I saw him
walking among the sick
   and infirm.
He spoke to them and
touched them, their hearts
   and lives.
And wonder of wonders,
they were healed, made whole!
And I marveled.

I then saw him
sending missionaries
   around the world.
He spoke of wisdom
found only in the hearts
   of the just and righteous,
and of the joy about to come,
   and everlasting peace,
    brotherhood

And I believed.

When last I saw him
he lay dead, felled by
    an assassin's bullet.
He died because the world
lay in disbelief and
    hatred; unwilling
to listen to the simple truth
    he proclaimed,
or to heed his words.
And I wept.

Someday the world
will love and know
    that great man of faith.
They will believe
    and all the peoples
        laud his name.
I await that glorious day,
and I pray.

As It Should

It should not always be that way.
    Times are hard.
      Things are bad.
For there is no perfect out,
no solution good enough.
And so we live
    from day to day
often asking why we struggle so.
    There is no gain,
      for all is lost.
But in our time we find at last
    a little love,
      someone we need,
      someone who needs us.
So we prove once again,
    life is good and all goes on
      as it should.

Sometimes I Wonder

Sometimes I wonder if death is nothing other than sleep.
Yes, death is just a short, simple sleep from which
each individual eventually awakens.
And when we awaken, we awaken at the beginning of another
dream of life: we are entirely different individuals.
Surely life is but a dream, a whim
that occurs in someone's mind.
Yes, someone, somewhere beyond the universe,
is dreaming ... dreaming ...
We are merely a segment of that great dreamer's dream.
And the infinitely endless universe
with all her stars, planets, and life forms
is nothing but a segment of the dreamer's dream.
I do not know how else to explain death,
for death cannot be explained easily, if at all.
But, sometimes I wonder.

I Love You, Girl

I love you, girl.
You're my bright and shining pearl,
My brilliant morning star,
Just a cut above par.

I love you, girl.
only you, girl.
I love you from now and for ever and ever,
I love you from now until never and never.

I love you, girl.
You set my mind and heart a twirl
With you there's no regret.
You're my one certain bet.

I love you, girl.
Only you, girl.
I love you from now and for ever and ever,
I love you from now until never and never.

I love you from now and for ever and ever,
I love you from now until never and never.
I love you, girl,
Only you, girl.
I really love you.

Poet's Lament

My mind's a blank.
That is quite a shame, too.
I was really wanting
   to write some verse
that would be immortalized.
No such luck.
Poetry is something
that evades my pen.
I write groups of phrases,
not beautiful poetry.
Alas!

Someday I will write
   the great, famous poem.
At least I hope to.
Only time will tell
   what's to be
Thus my lament --
a poet seeking a poem.

Afterthoughts

And now another chore
Has come unto my door.
And though it's not a bore
I think I know more.

Is this collection of words
Something for the birds?
I dare say no, no!
It's something all should know.

I see the bumble bee
Flying 'neath an apple tree
All for the sake of honey,
Good for you and me.

Someday it may rain
To green the dried plain.
Until that good time
I'll drink my lemon-lime.

In A Plain Paper Wrapper

It came to me
   in a plain paper wrapper.
I marveled at the wonder,
and thought of old dreams,
   unmade hopes and plans
that can't come true.
I could not ask why,
   where I failed,
   or even how.
The act was written
and I played the fool.
The future was there
   though not as bright
    as it might have been.
And still I believed
and hoped and dreamed.
Good dreams they were.
And I saw them
   in a plain paper wrapper.

Year's End Message

As the fading year ends
It's good to think of friends
And marvel at fortune good
With all the blessings one should.

With the start of another year
It's great to spread good cheer.
And wish our friends a special blessing
One marked with greatest stressing.

So I say to you, my friends,
Until all eternity ends,
Merry Christmas and Happy New Year,
For I hold your friendship dear.

Little Dog Lost

Little dog lost,
what cruel fate
   has cast you out
   without a home or future?

Maybe you're not lost
   but rather are
   a cast-off
     from a once happy home.
Cruel was the human
   who loved you and
   then cast you off
     as one would a
     battered rag doll.

Perhaps someday man may learn
   to treat all creatures as
   he himself would like
     to be treated.
Until then you remain --
   little dog lost.

I Don't know

Today is said to be great.
I don't know.
And man must never hate.
I don't know.

People come and go
And shouldn't we know
That after a season
We'll know the rhyme and reason.
"What is truth?" we ask.
This question's the task
Of life, and then
We wonder once again.

Children have the answers all.
Do we listen? Not at all.
It lies in simple faith in life
Free from cares and useless strife.
What do children have? Love.
What do children show? Love.

Someday we'll know
How to tell and show
Love for one another.
Kindness toward our brother.

Until the time that love abounds,
We shall live like baying hounds.
Today is said to be great.
I don't know.
And love is seldom late.
I don't know.

A Rainy Day

Gray and drab,
dismal and depressive,
melancholy and morose
are words of description.
They bespeak gloom
and cry out, 'despair'.
These words speak the truth
on the point in discussion,
and aptly describe – -
a rainy day.

All Too Human

Our world is growing old.
She's scarred and wrinkled,
    blind and crippled.
All this and more
    but not without
        reason.

The news we read in
    papers and magazines
and hear on the radio
    or see on television
        is negative.
We hear of corruption,
    violence, greed,
    envy, jealousy,
    prejudice,
        and a score of others.
Then we ask why.

The reason is simple;
we fear involvement.
'It's not my concern,'
    is the slogan of today.
Thus we speak
    and slowly turn away.

If all the world's a stage,
   and this is true;
our play is much the
   tragedy.
Or maybe we play
   the comedy of errors.
This must be so,
   for we accept our part
    and then perform.

We should stand united
   in our war for human dignity.
Treat all men as equals
   and as brothers
   should be the rule.
And so,
   let's open up our
    hearts and minds;
let's live in love
   and harmony,
    before the world
     dies of old age.

So The Ends Came

And so the ends came.
Not because we wanted them
    but because that was
        what was dictated.
Life is raw
and full of adventure.
    But there is no choice.
What we have and
    what we are
        is destined to be.

If we could change all,
    we would.
But because we don't,
    we cannot.
No beginnings here.
All lies in the end.
    And time passes.
Tomorrow may be better.
If only we could try,
    we could live free.

It is all impossible.
We have been set
    like a clock.
That is the way.
        So the ends came.

Poets

Poets
seem to be out of
fashion this year.
No one is wearing them.
They say things no one
wants to hear.
Poets talk and
no one, but poets,
pauses to listen;
they write and
no one reads.
So pathetic it seems.

There must be more
to life than sorrowing
over lost causes.
But I don't know what.

The Devil's Circus

And so we live in fear.
It could be worse, but I
   don't see how.
Tonight is like a dream of chance.
With the dawn is a new world.
Perchance a world of hope,
   but most likely one of dread,
      like all our yesterdays.
So we live.
   And so we live.

Negative.
   So be it if that's all there is.
Is it so?
If not negative,
   where is the positive?
In our sleep, our dreams,
   or perhaps in our waking?
No!
We make our lives, for better or for worse.
And don't be fooled by lies
   for we all lie and remain liars
      until the end.
Is life then hell?
   Heaven?

Who's to say? Where is the answer?
Look about, friend, and behold,
    the answer comes.

The answer.
    The answer lies in deeds
        and plans, thoughts and actions.
And in words spoken and written.
By man or by spirit?
Spirit.
That is our dream of hope.
    Let us not lose it.

Which Home?

The country is beautiful.
Mountains, streams, rivers, valleys,
    all bespeak the beauty,
        the grandeur of the area.
This place could become home.

But thoughts return to childhood
    days and a warmth is
kindled within the breast.
Memories come of the first home,
    the first love of life.
And a desire forms to return
to the place known so very well.

To be torn between two homes is terrible.
One home must ultimately prove
    more homey than the other.
The decision must be made:
    Where does the heart really lie?
    In my first home!
There is peace, there is joy, there
hope lies and faith dwells among
    friends and special places.

Workers' Lament

The clock is ticking merrily along.
I wish it wouldn't.
Soon I'll have to work again.
Work is a frustrating experience;
not nearly enough breaks.
Why,
   there should be
   at least one break
      every five minutes.
And the breaks should be
   at least ten minutes
      in length.

Don't get me wrong,
I'm not lazy,
   I just don't like to work.
Who does, after all?
You might, if you're
   a little light upstairs.
Some are.
   Pity.

It has been said that
   if people didn't work
   nothing would ever

get done.
That must be so.
Also we couldn't eat
   without money.
And money doesn't come
   without work.

Pity.

Alfalfa

Alfalfa is an interesting
    crop.
It adds more to the soil
    than it
      subtracts.
Interesting indeed!

Isn't it a pity that man,
who takes away from but
    returns little to
      nature,
doesn't take a lesson
    from the alfalfa?

Dracula

Silently on black wings he flies
seeking some luckless soul
who ventures out at night.
What hell unleashes his terror
is a question unanswered.
There is no hope but a
rugged cross and stake
for the hunter and his victims.
Peace will only come in death
for the morbid undead
amongst the living.
Thus lives the vampire.

Werewolf

The legend of the darkest age
    is here to haunt us still.
The creature, the beast,
    has come to maim and kill.
Half man, half wolf, who comes
    when the moon is full.
The rages have not changed;
the horror comes to pull
our souls to the blackest pit.
The werewolf returns again.

A Truth

The times are treacherous!
Uncertainty greets us at
   each and every door,
and nowhere seems
the surety of our lives
   tomorrow.
What lies ahead?
   Where will we be?
      What will we do?

Life is full of tricks
   and treachery
of deceitful man.
They would rob us of our souls
   if only they could.
Heaven knows they rob us
   of all our earthly possessions.
Maybe the lesson we can learn
from life is not to run
   from troubles,
     but rather,
meet them as they come
and master them.
After all,
We are the masters of our destiny!

A Present State of Affairs

I have spoken secrecies,
things of silence and mystery.
By secrets of the mind
to say ideas which no one
else can share.
Dreams of peace and
   worldwide love
are my secrecies
stated in verse,
shared by no one.

The world has no use for
   wise men.
It listens only to fools
who mislead and serve
   with treachery.
A lie spoken is taken
   for truth;
truth is a necessary falsehood.
Thus lies the state of affairs,
   the state of mind.

My words mean nothing really.
I, too, am a fool with thoughts
   which mislead.

Never Is Forever

Never is forever, or so it seems.
All our yesterdays have paved the way
for what is today.
And today forms our tomorrows.
Sorrows come and then they go.
So it is with happiness.
Only we remain;
enclosed in our shells
from which we never leave.
Thus we spend our days
in pity and false hopes
always seeking the release
which eludes our grasp.
Thus life – - an endless procession
of events over which we have no control.
From now until forever.
Never is forever.

I Guess

Oh, why does he say
In his most quaint way
To write another poem?
In order to go home
I must try to do
What's said to me and you.

But, I guess it's right
To take a pen and write
Words to a blank page
And end famous in an age
Or so. Who knows
How the wind blows?

It's all right, I guess,
To do this and bless
His heart and soul.
It's like a big bowl
Of chicken gumbo.
I guess his name is Bimbo.

To My Friend

It is rough being an adult.
Things never seem quite so simple
   as they did when we were young.
Life is hard.
We cannot always have those things
   we would wish.
But we must never despair,
   for there is always hope,
      and family and friends
     who care, who love, who are
        willing to share and help carry
        our burdens and despair.
We must always believe in ourselves
and count our mistakes and failures
   as steps toward our perfection.
Only believe!
   By believing we will succeed.
     Only believe!
        And you cannot fail.

Fond Day

The days were long and harsh,
    but we had joy and love.
Hate was something only dreamed,
a passing fancy never to be shared.
Fate had other ideas,
    for we were to be controlled
        by events beyond our control.
Thus, the never-ending story
    of life and strife,
and all that breeds discontent.
Discontent came only as a means
    of escape from reality, drudgery.
But we knew all was not yet lost,
for always was there tomorrow
    with its hopes and aspirations.

Come, fond day, tomorrow and
    bring peace.

Life Is But a Fantasy

Life is but a fantasy, a dream,
   a mist full of shadows.
Nowhere is anything real, all is sham.
What power then dreams?
   Can all that we perceive be nothing?
And if not true and substance,
   then all is make believe.
Colors are without shade, forms
   without solidarity.
Fantasies are the conceptions of the future.
   Tomorrow is not there to touch.
   All we have is today and the longing
     to keep what was yesterday.
My mind spins with contemplation
and can be sure of emptiness.
Why is there life and love, and hope?
   For all is fantasy.

What Madness Is This

What madness is this that I should feel afraid
    of the dark and unknown, all I don't understand?
What mental blocks have I set in my mind
    because I haven't taken the time to learn?
After all the time of darkness, is only the time of
peace, rest and hopeful contemplation.
        All is well and as it should be.
I am a man, a frail creature of habit,
    with passions and ignorance.
My heart is vain.

Understanding comes with knowledge;
    knowledge comes from caring and a willingness
        to learn, to love and to live
            and let live.
My madness comes from turning my back on all
    I see and perceive.
Nothing ventured is nothing gained, so I remain
    shallow, hollow, and utterly mad.
That is why my cry of:

    What madness is this!

Whoever You Are

Whoever you are, I want you to know
    that you are my friend.
And this I say although we have never met.
The thought is not as strange as it seems;
    I love people, all people,
        rich and poor, the famous and unknown.
People.
    Yes that is where life and adventure dwells.
People.
    The force behind all experience and thought
        and wonder.

I have met you.
    In my dreams, in my fondest desires, in my
        hopes and aspirations.
You are my friend and trusted companion.
And this even though we have not met.
    We will meet someday, this is sure,
        and all I think and dream will be.
I love you, friend,
    whoever you are

A Beautiful Day

There must be a secret
    in a beautiful day.
The wind blows,
the leaves rustle,
the grass waves,
and the air holds
    a sweetness.
Perhaps it's nothing,
but there is a quality
in beauty.
    Certainly a day has it.

Blue sky and sunlight
make the earth seem bright.
And at night there appear
    twinkling stars
which shatter the blackness.
At such moments as those
    experienced while looking
    for mysterious things,
all is serenity.
Color imprints are beautiful
    to the minds' eye.
And the day has many colors.

We only need look
for what is there.
Yes.
There must be a secret
in a beautiful day.

Wish Upon A Star

If I could wish upon a star
and have my wish come true
I wonder what I'd wish.
Fame and fortune
   would be nice,
     as would be power.
But the best wish by far
would be to meet,
   get to know, and befriend
     all people everywhere.
Friendships are more valuable
than all the wealth of the world.
So great friendships
   would be my wish
   upon a star.

Some Still Call Him Pig

I saw him cry.
It was there beside the road.
   The tears came unbidden,
    unashamedly.
He wept for a loss,
   a great loss –
    the death of a child,
an innocent, run over
   by a drunk driver.

I saw him weep.
It was as he carried
   the boy to the
    shaded playground.
He cried out of his
   heartfelt compassion
    and love for all children --
children living in an unsure
   unsafe world.

Who would believe or
   even understand
    such actions from a cop.

But his lot is to
　　serve and protect.

What more could be said.
　　His kindness, his goodness,
　　　　shone through.
And some still call
　　him "pig."

Stranger in the Mirror

Look in the mirror
   and who do you
see?
A stranger.
Someone completely alien,
   some unknown
person
stares back.
And this, seemingly
   strange,
is nothing out of the
   ordinary.
It is rather the fact
   that we
are strangers unto
   ourselves.
Thus, man.

Insomnia

You attack me in the night
    with an urgent restlessness.
I pace and think,
    sometimes pouring over
      that good book,
    all to no relief.

Perhaps television can
    bring the dream,
where words and the count
    of sheep cannot.

      Alas!

It is all to no avail.
    And so I roam the quiet,
      deserted streets
hoping beyond hope
    for that glorious
      and often wished for entity.

    Sleep!
      Blessed sleep!

Maybe now.

Id

The moon is high
And devils cry
All in the land if Id.
Monsters roar
And witches soar
All in the land of Id.
Werewolves howl
And vampires prowl
All in the land of Id.
Zombies walk
And ghouls stalk
All in the land of Id.
Ghosts groan
And spirits moan
All in the land of Id.
Land of Id.
Land of Id.
Dreaming _is_ the land of Id.

Thoughts of Darkness

There's something about the night
   which haunts the soul.
It seems as though all
the childhood fears and terrors
   are drawn across the mind.
A breeze rustles the leaves
and ghosts appear,
   if only for a second.
Evil lurks where man dares
   not tread.
Such thoughts linger with the dark,
only to be dispelled by the light.
And all seems as if a dream.
But night always returns,
   bringing that secret dread,
   the shadow, the whisperer
     in darkness.
And we wonder why.
And we wonder.
   Why?

Memory

I think of my life
   and all that once was.
Can it really be past?
   Is it all yesterday,
      and yesterday's gone?

I look at my life
   and I seemingly only lived
      in the past.
I'm locked in the fifties
   and perhaps the sixties.

My people were alive then,
   All is now a corner
      of emptiness, loneliness.
It cannot all be over.
   Surely not over.

There is tomorrow with
   all it's uncertainties.
Middle-age has its drawbacks.
   Too much caution seems
      the norm.

Can my life really
   be past?

Never! Never!
   I know I shall always
      be.

Rocks

Behold the rock.
It sits on its throne
   from day to day,
unmovable, without passion,
    parts.
The life it leads is dull.
No chance to become
   other than worthless sand.
     Tragic.

I have known men
   who were hard
   to move –- no feelings.
Just like the rock.
They live from day to day
   never thinking about
   other men on the way.
And all because their hearts
   are stone:
objects without love.
    A tragedy, this.

Wind

Who knows the wind?
The wind cannot be known –
   as such –
      but it can be felt
      and heard as it moves scenery.
No odor marks its presence,
   but it spreads a certain
   scent of rose petals
   passed through on its way.
The wind represents freedom
   in the truest sense of words.
It cannot be bound or stopped.

Men should also be so free that
   they are never chained
      or oppressed.
Someday that time of peace
   may come.
Until then, the wind blows
   and bespeaks
      peace and freedom.

Times

Yesterday was wonderful!
I enjoyed the good, happy times
we shared together as friends.
Yes, we were quite happy,
    if happiness comes
    from living free
    and enjoying each other's
        company.
Good times they were.

Today is really no different
    than all our yesterdays.
Friendships remain like sentinels
    protecting us from emotions
    of hate, mistrust, greed.
It would seem that today
    is just an extension of yesterday.
All is happiness.

Tomorrow will no doubt come
bringing us contentment in old age.
Our lives flash before us like dreams
    in the night which bespeak fiction.
Nothing is real in old age
But that is …
    tomorrow.

Exiled Emotion

Where does love begin?
With a smile?
In a nod?
In a spoken word?
In a friendly gesture?
When hearts rejoice
at sharing company?
Friends feel more than
they say.

It seems strange
that love's origin
cannot be found
in definitions.
Words are cold, unfeeling.
Men are not.

Because I am a man
let me love my friends,
and not be afraid to express my feelings
as so many do.

Wyoming Interlude

I spent a week in Cokeville.
A week, give or take
   a couple of days.
It seemed like an eternity.
I had nothing to do,
   I knew no one.
I had, then, a vague idea
of sinking my roots
in that little Wyoming corner.

No such luck.

I locked myself in
   room two
at the Stockman Hotel.
Twenty dollars a week –
   a reasonable price
seeing that the hotel had
   outlived the wild west.
Antique.
In any case I got my
money's worth.

Job prospects didn't come
    my way.
I didn't look too hard.
I just thought it might
    be good to go home.
Wyoming is a goodly
distance from Kansas.
And this in all shades
    of life
as well as climate.

Cokeville citizens were friendly.
This as though they cared
    about you and had always
        been your friend.
(Such was also the case
    in the Ozarks –
    but that was long ago.)
I wondered why this was so.

Are all the small,
    story-book places
the only ones so friendly?
That seems the case,
    though it's really strange.
I wonder, still, why this is so.

Fun and Games and Party Favors

When young I had no cares;
all was fun and games and party favors.
Laughter was my soul
    and life's inspiration.
I was content and at peace
    with the world and myself.

Years passed, flew by
    it seemed.
And then, before I knew
    what had happened,
I was all grown up.

With the passing years
    and the coming of age
    my laughter died
to be replaced by sadness,
    worries, dreams,
    and endless sorrow.
Hopes aspired only to be
    crushed and destroyed.
The call rang true:
fun and games and party favors.

I listened to the news
and saw evil, discontent,
    hatred everywhere;
then dreamed dreams of peace.
They were but dreams,
    nothing more.

The news once again spoke.
Now there were countless disasters.
Another test bomb was dropped
    killing the human race slowly.
Political systems were struggling
    to dominate the earth,
and religious wars were being
    started and lost by all.
Again the cry went forth:
fun and games and party favors.
No hope …
    and I dreamed dreams
        of peace.

I attended the churches
and listened to their sermons.
Corruption even prevailed in
    sanctuaries of God.
Oh, they believed they were right!
Every Sunday they met and had
fun and games and party favors.
All for the demand
    of the congregation.

I saw these things –
    looked in awe—
and wondered what is the truth.
Truth must lie in wait

for those who seek
    her wisdom.
But we must look carefully
    or our search is ended …
       lost.

"Hope for man,
    where are you?
Why do you not answer?"
This was my cry
    unto the heavens.
Still no answer was to be had.
The just and righteous had fled.
At least this is how it seemed.

What was wrong with me
    I did not know.
But I could do nothing
    short of surrender
until that day I was alone
    and afraid
and I found the Book.
I read the words
    and marveled.
Here at last I had
    found the truth
    and the light.
"A cause at last!"
became my cry.
This was hope and love
found in but a book,
    the Book.

I knew man had not been forgotten.
Someone cared – enough.
Salvation.

And thus was ended all
fun and games and party favors.

I Am a Seeker

I am a seeker.
Please invite me in
when I knock at your door,
for my visit will prove very rewarding
for you if you do.
   I will be thirsty,
      give me drink.
   I will be hungry,
      give me bread.
I will be naked,
      give me clothes.
   I will be lonely,
      give me companionship.
Your reward will be peace, hope, joy,
and, most of all, love:
the love of a lonely heart.
This is the greatest reward which can be bestowed
upon any individual.
Cherish it as you would your own body.
Yes,
I am a seeker; you are a finder.

Pale Horse

I rode a pale horse
from coast to coast and
never asked why the ride,
but moved on steadily.
I thought the same trip
might have been easier,
   more enjoyable.
I didn't know, however,
it would have been
   more adventurous.
It's just impossible --
a pale horse is vicious.
I received sores, bruises, and burns
accompanied by scorn
as I wandered through country
spotted with valleys, mountains, and plains.
And as I traveled
I knew it was no new journey,
though it could only be accomplished once.
Now I know life is such --
   a pale horse:
I must ride as all,
   until my journey's end.

This Valentine's Day

Of course again it's time for valentines.
It happens once a year.
   And as the fleeting years roll by
     acquaintances are brought to mind.
With the memory a sense of loss,
   for in our daily living
     we oft times forget the
     caring and sharing
  of friends and those we hold
      so dear.
And moments lost are never gained.
   We lose the experience of watching
  and living with the ones
    around us.
For the moments lost –- the shadows in time –-
   I must repent.
     I must learn to give,
     and care, and share.

With this new beginning
  and understanding
I must say today,
  this Valentine's Day,

    Be my valentine,
     be my friend.

R.I.P.

He was such a good man,
    my cousin,
though he didn't seem
    a saint.
He led a trying life.
Things just didn't
    work out for him:
        nothing in his favor.
Oh, he tried his best,
it just wasn't any good.
Now he's gone.

The world seems full of
    pathetic people.
But what is to be done
    for them, what
    can we do?
I suppose we must
learn to live with them.
We will do nothing
    for them.
It's not our way.

Middle of a Heat Wave

Oh, how it was hot
   that day
   last summer!
The trees seemed to
   melt
as though they were
   chocolate.
But they didn't really.
It just seemed so
   in the heat.

That was the day
   Charles drowned;
the middle of a heat wave.
Some said Charles
   just had a
swimming mishap.
But he was fully clothed
   and had an anchor
tied to his waist.
Murder?
   Hardly.
Charles was just tired
   of life.

It's a pity really --
    so many suicides.
We must not let
    ourselves
become so discouraged
and beaten down,
    that we take
        such a drastic
        step.

Charles needed faith;
    in himself if
        nowhere else.

Have faith:
    live abundantly.

Dark Corner

We have a dark corner
    in our lives,
        you and I.
We have stumbled
    somehow along
the way.
It's strange, almost
    unnatural
the way we fell into
our dark corner.
It started with
    mistrust.
Now there is
    misunderstanding.
Love,
let us strive to find
    our way out
before it's too late.
We are one,
    you and I.

The Survivors

A strange family,
    that.
The old man just
    passed away
and they seek to divide
his widow's wealth.
Family unity there
    has faded.
All that remains
    is greed,
        lust,
            hatred.
I wonder what's
    in store
for those who remain,
    the survivors.

The Wind at Our Back

The wind at our back,
that's the way we have it.
The world turns and leaves us behind,
but as long as there is the wind at our back,
    we exist in part.
There is no death,
Only the ceaseless breezes out of time
    which carry us away into a new existence:
Life, love and hate, joy and sorrow,
the end of existence.
And, always,
the wind at our back.

An Apple A Day

I once heard the saying,
"An apple a day
keeps the doctor away,"
But this just cannot
   be so.
Apples make me ill.
Sayings can often
   be misleading.
They stress someone's
   idea
rather than the
   factual.

More Thoughts

The green grass of spring
is like unto
   a goddess
of infinite love.
She fascinates each mortal
   with her promise
   of eternal life.
Grass lives into
   infinity.
But man is mortal.
Is he really mortal though?
Is there a life
   after death?
Who is He who
   knows?
Perhaps the grass
   is not a
   goddess
but proof of a life
   after death.
Believe.

I Am Not Afraid of Death

I am not afraid of death.
What is there in death to fear?
Death is not the end, but the beginning:
There is a life after death.
And even if there were no life after death,
death would still be nothing to fear,
for in death we can at last find peace.
When in death we no longer suffer or feel pain,
all our troubles and worries are left behind,
our spirit or soul goes on to greater things.
We shall not want,
for we are in the care of our Parents.
Death is a necessary end
and therefore, should not be feared.
So why be afraid?
There is a life after death.
I am not afraid of death.

A Statement in Effect

I wonder if friendship
   is worth all the pain and trouble.
I suffer for my friends
   when they feel pain or sorrow.
I weep with them
   in times of remorse.
I sacrifice for them,
   my friends,
and often neglect myself.

It really isn't too much
   on my part.
I just wonder if I do enough.

Some call me fool.
But those people don't
   know me.
They cannot understand.

I do all for my friends
and ask nothing in return.
Gratitude is in feelings;
   I love my friends.

Point of Interest

I marvel at all that's strange.
If it's different
   and out of the ordinary
I find a deep interest
   within my soul
      which compels me.
I must know all there is to know
   about the subject.

And after a time
I know the strangeness is gone.
I understand,
   I perceive,
and realize that nothing
   was really different
      or unusual.
The strangeness made the subject unique.

If the subject
   of my observation
is unique,
then all is one
   and as it should be.

I Am A Comedian

I am a comedian,
one of the loneliest men in the world.
I make others laugh at and with me,
but I cannot make them laugh for me.
I am loved and followed because I am humorous,
not because I am a man.
To my admirers I am an object –
something that is to be used now and later discarded.
But this is not what I want!
I want to belong, to be accepted
because I am an individual and not an item.
Admit, accept, love.

Bible

I used to think
   that God
was hidden;
   out of sight,
     out of sound.
But then I came
   to realize
my error.
God is real,
   His word is that shield,
   that sword, that lance
which protects us
   as we journey
on the road
   of life.

Quest

God is love!
   Perhaps,
who's to say?
You can't be sure,
   though
you try.
Maybe life itself
   is love.
But, this can't be so;
it destroys your
   belief
in God.
The truth is there;
it's just hidden
until you love.
   God is real.

Testimony

Testimony.
  It lives in my heart
  and expands my thinking.
Testimony,
  is all I live for
  and all I hope to see.
Testimony is truth.
  It comes from within
  and strengthens the soul.
Testimony,
grants me freedom
  to do all that is right,
    and wisdom to
    confront all opposition.
Testimony is my shield,
  my sword,
  and the iron rod
    to cling to in
    these troubled times

The Thought

A voice sounds —-
words spoken,
and a tale is presented.
Each sentence tells a story
    fascinating enough
    for a best seller.

People.
They are the ones who speak.
And in speaking tell
    the unwritten stories.
Stories which should be told
    but seldom are.
Pity that.

Existence is loneliness.
We are truly alone.
And yet,
    loneliness begets
    friendships, brotherhood.

Tales are often told
    out of lone ideas and men.
Thus we gain wisdom.

Wheat

Often we see
the green and yellow
    sea of wheat
blowing in the summer breeze
and smell its perfect
    odor after a
rain shower.
We sometimes
wonder what makes it
so change.
One day it's
    green
and fresh,
the next, it's turning
    yellow;
and we know harvest
is just around
    the corner.
We sense a little
sadness at its
parting.
Almost a friend
    is the familiar
wheat.

He Who Digs A Grave

A man
living from day to day,
never asking why,
    little caring,
is he who digs a grave.

It makes no difference
how he tries to change
    things,
all remains the same.

A man walking
down the street
sees a crime
    being committed,
but never cares,
    never gets involved.

Apathy.
When apathy rules,
society dies.
Such a society
    is a conglomeration
        of dead people.
And this because of
    he who digs a grave.

To Friendship Lost

I walk the silent streets
    of loneliness,
always looking back
into the chasms of the past,
    for you.
You are there,
hidden by shadows
    out of time,
obscured by the haze
which clouds memory.

I cannot remember enough.
    Good times.
        Happy times.
            Past times.
And I cannot return.
All is lost,
    save blurred images
    of memory.

And what of the future?
There can be no future
    with your loss,
save the bleak prospect
of a world of solitude
    without you, beloved friend,
    without you …

Labor Day '71

We waded up the
  Smokey Hill
didn't we, my friend?
It was something,
  fun perhaps,
to wade in the mud and slime
and bruise our naked feet on the
  sandy bottom.
And just to be there with you
  was a thrill.

Ah, my young friend,
  shall we wade again?

The Old Hotel

The old hotel
    stands on the corner
saddened by time,
    and remembers
    good times.
It looks so mournful
    as you pass,
that you feel it has
    a heart;
breaking with misuse, age.
So decrepit now
    the old hotel.
Gone.

Stonehenge

We wonder what mysteries
those ancient stones
    could tell.
They stand in defiance
    of modern science.
And this, not intentional,
but as a result of their being:
a secret of ages past,
    a marvelous work
    created at the hand
    of ancient man.
Thus,
    Stonehenge.
Perhaps science will never
unlock the secret of the stones,
    but this is sure – -
the intelligence that erected
    the fabulous wonder
    is greater than our own.

Everybody Gets Hit in the Mouth Sometime

I asked you to marry me.
    I loved you.
    I worshiped you.
However, you said you had
much more of life
        to live
before you were ready to
    settle down.

I can understand
    that at nineteen
you wanted to explore
        your world.
    I did also
        at nineteen.
But you shattered my world
    with your refusal.
Now I am ready to die.

I just hope you never
        suffer sorrow
        as I now do.
    But then,
everybody gets hit in the mouth sometime.

Colors

Thoughts of blue invade the mists
   of action,
undreamed plans and deeds.
Nothing is peaceful, green.
And that's sad.
Crimson glimpses come
   and go, but
blue remains as a token
   of sadness.
Yellow and brown
   seem real at times.
But,
   they, too,
     are drowned out
     by blue ideas of shadows.
Black and white
   never enter the picture;
they are opposite ends of
   the spectrum.
Only blue counts and
   conquers.
Reason evades the mind
   leaving colors –– blue.

Skinny-dipping

We went skinny-dipping together
  many times.
It was thrilling, fun perhaps,
to feel the sun rays
  and warm summer breezes
    on our naked bodies.
The feel of the cool water
against our skin as we swam.
  The mud and sand oozing
    between our toes
as we waded the slimy shallows
was exciting.
The river banks were oh
so warm as we lay
  drying off and sunning
    ourselves.
Mother Nature was good to us.
Skinny-dipping was a joy.

Riches

Possessions can be evil.
This, when we cleave to them
   as we would gold and silver.
Evil seeks to destroy
all that is good.
Things of this world;
   there lies our fate.
All is chance in a world
   of great riches.
Wealth and earthly possessions
   are things for which we lust.
Little can we hope to
   gain heavenly light
   when so-called
      Christian virtues
      are nonexistent.
A truth revealed.
Thus it is with possessions
   of the world.

Let Us Now Praise Famous Men

Let us now praise famous men!
The hired man, the farm hand
who makes his bread by the
   sweat of his brow.
He toils long, hot, hard
hours performing
   back-breaking,
   muscle straining
     labor.
His burden is not light
   in life.
His hands are callused
   and misshapen
from years of abuse
   brought on by his
     tasks.
May the hired man, the farm hand
   be blessed with joy
   and abounding pleasures
in the afterlife.
He deserves a reward,
   the famous man.
     So.
Let us now praise famous men!

That's Life

Someday I may be rich.
Then I can have all I want.
Even then I'll probably
want more than I have.
And I'll be where I am now,
reaching for the sun.
Then, that's life.

In Memoriam

Peter Christian Andersen

An elderly gentleman
aged four score and six
when he said his farewell.
He was a heavy-set man – to heavy
for the bathroom scale.
A man with a head of gray and white hair
that now showed no sign of once being black.
He had a round face that
clearly showed the lines
of age and a life of worry.
Few men could withstand
the pressures of life he once faced.
He worked hard as a carpenter
during the depression years
to support his family.
He planned for four children,
and received twelve.
He accepted the responsibility,
however, and raised the twelve
making them respectable citizens.
He had a sense of humor
that even worries could not falter.
He became childish in later
life and caused much heart-ache.
But he loved and was loved
and is now greatly mourned.

Grandma A.

Nina Eudora MarKell Andersen;
   Such a gentle lady – never one
   to raise her voice, or complain
    about anything.
She loved her family more than
   life itself. Knitting and
    crocheting were her
   hobbies, as was quilting.
As a cook, she was beyond
    compare.
Often she could be found working
   in her flowerbeds.
    She had a green thumb –
anything she planted would grow.
    She said her farewell in 1976
    at the age of ninety.
I will always miss her;
    my Grandma A.

The Trio

I see them still, in my mind's eye.
    Sisters.
  I remember the stories,
and my mind creates a panorama.

There were trips after all had
    graduated. And it seems
      so strange that the youngest
        always ended up the driver.

      There were the photographs.
Taken on the spur of the moment
or posed in an atmosphere of seriousness.
      One pose stands out above
      the rest – the youngest posing
      on the hood of the car as
        Bonnie Parker.

They had such good times.

      War came and there was the
      U.S.O.
          Dances.

All for the war effort

Four brothers went to war —
And all returned.
Sisters — all are gone now.
There is so much to be remembered,
and much is lost.
Their story needs to be told.

The trio.
The eldest was my mother,
the younger two, aunts.
Though they may now be gone,
They live in my memory,
and laugh, and love,
and are.
Leola, Dorothy, Florence.

Markings

I met a man once.
He left behind, when he died,
a few markings.

I think he had a fame
about him.
Because of his simple
markings.

Some called him author.
Philosopher would suffice.
He saw reality in dreams
and left markings.
Tales, true, these markings,
but more than fables.
They captured a picture
of life, love.

Simple were the markings.
The man became legend.

Bobby

I see him still,
    the hero, the young gladiator,
as he fought to achieve
    a great destiny.
But that destiny was not to be.
His destiny lay in
    anguish, tears,
        and death.

It seems all the great heroes
do not get the chance to fulfill
    their potential promise.
Their time ends so abruptly,
    usually at the hands of
        an assassin.
And so it was with Bobby,
the young gladiator,
    the hero.

All he wanted was to stop
    a seemingly senseless war
which was taking the lives
    of so many young men
        with great promise.
Therefore he sought public office.

That young man, who given the chance,
    would have been the best of them all.
His life ended;
    ended so tragically,
but his dream lived on.
Peace.
    And the dream did
        become reality.

The man himself, the hero,
    the young gladiator
has joined the ranks
    of those destined
        to become legend.
And legend he is,
    and always shall be
as long as man sings
the annals of the great.

Bobby,
    we will never forget.

Sammy

I weep bitter tears
    when I think of you
and your untimely end.
    What was your sin,
        your crime
to warrant the piercing
    wound from behind?
And you just fourteen --
    still a boy.

I rage in the night
    and consider the
        injustice committed.
You
    who had hope
        and so much promise.
    Your life snuffed out
    by a protector.

My anguish is for you,
    your promise unfulfilled,
the generations truly lost;
    all for an act so
        unfair, so wrong.

Sammy, Sammy!

Richard

I see you in the dreams
   of yesterday, that time
      of joyful innocence;
a world of hope and schemes
   and great promise.

But the dream is now gone,
   replaced by a new reality,
      a glorious awareness.
In my heart I see you on
   the other side of the veil,
      being greeted by Dusty
and called to serve with him
   on an important, exalted mission.

The emptiness in my heart
   comes from knowing that
      no more in this life
will I hear your voice and laughter,
   and see your disarming,
      but mischievous smile.

And at your parting I will
   never, never say goodbye,
      but so long for now.

Death is not an end of existence
    but the threshold of a new beginning.
We will speak together again, my friend.
    Every fiber of my being tells
      me this is so.
So until we meet again,
    Richard, my friend, my friend,
      so long and farewell for now.

Country Boy

When I heard the news
   I was deeply saddened.
The curtain had come down
   on another of my favorite people.
Fifty-three, such a short time.

You spoke through your
   music and songs
with such a gentle voice.
Your message touched my heart
   and touched my soul.

You sang of mountains and lands,
   of people and home, and love.
You spoke of caring and sharing
   and loving all as brothers.

Too much has passed.
   Too much is lost.
Though lost, never forgotten,
   no, never, never, forgotten.
Through the music and
   message of your songs
there is the truth –
   you are eternal and will

surely never die.

John, my heart cries –
   I loved you and will
      always, always, miss you.
Country boy, singer,
   this is a farewell for now,
      not goodbye.
I will never forget.

Tommy

He was just a boy
  when he left us.

It seems like so long ago
  we changed his diapers
    and wiped his nose.

Time passed.

There was little league and
  soccer and football.
It was the time of skinned knees
  and bruised shins and elbows.
Band-Aids were his mark of life.

Again time passed.

High school came and
  became an adventure.
There were the games and plays,
the classes and dances.
And most important, graduation.

And time passed.

The country, our country,
    called, and he went.
        So proud to serve.

The telegram came today.
Your son was killed on Hill Nine.
    He was a brave lad.

He was just a boy
    when he left us.
        Our son … Tommy

Ricky

I remember him.
I cannot forget.
He was a singer,
    a teen idol,
but very much a strong
    memory out of my past.

He sang about
a girl named Mary Lou
    and a travelin' man
        and a garden party.
And to hear him sing
    gladdened the heart.
Such was the greatness
    of this wonderful,
        unique performer.

Besides singing he starred
    with his family on
    a weekly and favorite
        television show.
Always there were laughs
    and such good times.

Can it really be over?

Has the curtain been drawn
    a final time?
Does a tragic plane crash
    end his existence?
No.
    He lives in the hearts
        of his fans
and all who loved him.
Such as he can never die.

Ricky,
    until we meet again,
        … So long.

Alexei

Child of fate,
  heir to an empire,
    Grand Duke,
  beloved son and brother.
What cruel gods brought you
  to your knees
and slapped you with
  such vile betrayal?

You child, who did no wrong
  met with pain
    and suffering.
I close my eyes
  and see the blood.
  I feel the crippling
    hemophilia.
My heart cries with anguish
  and such deep despair.

I see your face before me
  in photographs and old
    motion pictures.
You, who were all boy
  despite your agony.
And compassion was
  in your heart.

This because of your pain.
Fleeting glimpses are
    all that remain
of your existence.
Though you were assumed murdered
    at thirteen, you live
        in my heart
and will never die.

Alexei, Alexei,
    Czarevitch.

Ryan

No more will I see his smile
   Or hear his voice and laughter
      for he is gone from us.
No longer will I feel his touch
   and gain strength from his embrace.
      He is now gone from us.

He suffered much pain and anguish
   during his sojourn here.
He was shunned and hated,
   called vile names,
      driven from his home.
And all because of a
   chance of fate,
      a disease called AIDS.

He fought for his rights.
   He refused to yield to others
      mistrust and fear.
To stand and live life
   to the fullest was
      his humble creed.

He won many friends
   through his lonely journey.

There were so very many
   who came to care, honor,
      and love him.
With his passing I sense
   a void which cannot
      be filled.
In him was so much hope,
   faith, love, promise.

Through all his trials and pain
   he never relinquished his trust
      and belief in God.
   So.
His trials are past.
   No more will he suffer,
   feel pain and anguish.
He is free to soar to worlds
   unknown but glorious,
He now walks with God.

For Dustin

Farewell, my friend, so long.
My heart aches at this parting,
   for your leave-taking came
      oh, so soon,
      way too soon.
Fifteen is too short a time
to experience all life's
   joys and thrills,
      laughter and loving.
And for all that,
your life touched mine
   and so many others.

I realize with your parting
   there is a void, and emptiness
      which cannot be filled.
One that seems far too real
   as you lay at rest today.

Although you are greatly mourned
   by those left behind;
sorrow and sadness will fade,
   tears will dry.
then will come the realization
   that you have been called

to a far more exalted sphere
where your spirit will soar
to heights unknown --
a more glorious mission.

And though you have parted from
this present existence,
your presence, your essence,
will live in our hearts
and will always remain
in memories and quiet thoughts,
joyful thoughts.

Farewell, my friend,
so long for now.
We, I, love you.

Family

Blessings of Family

The blessings of the family
  cannot be counted,
and yet, they are simple.
Love abounds and contentment
  reigns in serenity.
It's a church, the family,
and sanctified of God.
Blessed are all they who
  marry and raise
  fine families.
The heavens are theirs
  because they have found
heaven in family life - -
  the trials, the triumphs,
  the laughter, the crying,
  the caring, the sharing, all.
Heaven on earth,
  the family.
Blessed are the parents
  and the children
Blessed are the children
  and the parents.

Tina

Love was something I always
   felt had passed me by.
I dreamed, hoped, and
    wished upon a star.
      All to no apparent result.
And I wondered why; where had I
   missed my opportunities.

     Years passed,
a seemingly eternity of loneliness.
    I gave up all hope.

Then a change came my way.
It would seem someone had their
   eye on me.
    A special angel sent
   to ease my burden and
be my friend, and eternal companion.

Gone was my emptiness, my incomplete
   state of being.
    I was now complete,
    both body and soul.

So strange what a wife will
   make a man,
      My happiness knows no bounds;
     my joy is full.
My cup runneth over.
   I have my best friend and
     confidant.

Tina, My Special Angel

You are the one who
   is there for me,
the one who makes me strong.
I adore you and your
   gentle ways.
I don't know how you
   put up with me.

It is so hard to see you
   in pain or discouraged.
But now I can do for you.
   I can be your rock
     to stand on.
I can be your shield
from the storm.

Just remember,
   we are one and meant
     to be so.
We will hold each other up
   through thick and thin,

Just remember I adore you!
   You, Tina, are my
     Special Angel!

The Pest

Boy, do I remember the pest.
   He came around when I was
   but nineteen months old.
For the next eighteen years
   the pest was there – my shadow –
   whenever I would turn around.
     One would think he
     <u>was</u> my shadow!

Boy did we fight like
   cats and dogs. No matter
   what happened, he always got
me in trouble. Then there were the
   times the pest pretended to be
     hurt so badly I was the
     one who got upset and cried.

Many years passed and the pest and I
   were remembering our growing years.
   I mentioned how he was
such a pest wanting to be
wherever I went.

His comment was,
    "Of course I wanted to be with you.
    You were my hero!"
That comment made me feel
    oh, so very small.

He was not only a pest –
    he was my brother.

Nephew

I write these words for you,
　　my nephew, my pride,
　　　　my joy.
Knowing you has been an honor
　　perhaps the greatest blessing
　　　　of my life.

It seems like only yesterday
　　you came into my life
　　　　and changed me forever.
You gave me purpose.
I was so proud, you could
　　have been my son.

Years have gone, so fleetingly
　　it seems.
You have grown into
　　a young man.
I see your dreams and hopes,
and I know you will prosper.
　　The world is yours:
　　　　conquer it.

I write these words for you,
　　my nephew, my pride, my joy.

Grandchildren

Being a grandfather can be
   a lot of fun since
      grandfathers are simply
fathers without rules.

I remember when Daniel's kids
   were young.
I had so much fun hauling them
   in a wagon and wheelbarrow.
      Then there was trick or treating.
The oldest grandson has grown to
   be a fine young man who
      went on a mission for the church.
The others are turning out fine.
Watching them grow has been a blessing.

It was great fun taking Steven's
   kids to the park to play.
When Celeste told me I was her
   idea of what a grandfather should be –
I felt pride, since all I wanted to be
   was a grandfather like mine.

Now I have a great-grandson.
   I will be able to spoil him
      like the grandkids.

Joshua

I see him still
   the little baby boy with
   brown hair and blue eyes
     as I first met him.
He had a trace of freckles
across his nose
and a cute grin
   which would disarm anyone.
This face had already
bespoke a lad of
active disposition.
So he was.

That meeting was nine years ago,
when he was that baby.
Now at nine he is just as active,
   just as full of life and mischief
     as ever.
But he would not be who he is
   if he were not as he is.
I would have him no other way.
A bright grandson that one;
   and a fine boy to boot.
     Almost an angel.
And so he is,
   still Grandpa's boy.

Jace

Child
   with angelic
      face,
what joys dance
through your sweet
      head?
This is your life.
All fun and games.
Seriousness avoids
   your brow.
      No cares.
It must be fun
   being young,
      innocent, beautiful,
      and a boy.

      My great grandson.

Youthfulness of Youth

Mark's Poem

Mark Proud Mahaffey,
A goodly name like R. E. Lee.
And this, greatly fair
Belongs to the great somewhere.
And what's in a name
But love, joy, and the same
As those of old named Mark
Who on their trip did embark
In the legends of history?
And thus it may be
For this lad, Mark Proud Mahaffey.

Clark's Poem

There's a lad named Clark
Who'll someday make his mark
In this world wide
And he must never hide
From such a wonderful life
As his; even with its strife.
I know this proud boy
Will soon find great joy.
A happiness most grand
As a fine marching band.
He's sure to find a place
In life's greatest race.

Scott's Poem

Of thoughts, all's been said
And of words my mind's bled.
But still he says write
So, I guess I just might.

I wonder what they think,
These little ones who blink.
What's in their noble mind?
Are we too often left blind?

I sometimes think they're right;
That we might live in hope tonight.
It's what is often said
So we must never dread.

All too soon he'll be grown
And have to live a life that's blown.
A certain future it's not
For this young friend, Scott.

Scott's Poem II

Shall you play today
In your fine way?
Or will you deeply think
Of a destruction that's on the brink?
Only you know your plans
In a life as mixed as tumbled fans.
And so you live just and happy
O youth, named Scott Mahaffey.

Heidi

She smiled and then laughed.
And I felt better and gladdened
   by the thought that she
   loved and was loved.
Child she is.
But with a sparkle,
   a love of life,
      a deep set happiness
         some adults lack.
It is a wonder, a marvel
being a girl with dolls and
   dreams and schemes.
She loves – an angel in human form –
   A precious gift.

Anthony

He was there,
a boy with a bow and arrows,
trying to catch my attention.
He only wanted a little
    recognition.
Perhaps he thought
of himself as someone
    extra special.
This he was,
but not to me.
I didn't know him.

That was then,
a lifetime in the past.
Now he's fifty-two
and an old acquaintance.
The things he once thought
I now think and believe.
He is special!
Special people seem
    to draw many friends.
That one does.

What more can I say
if not that I love him
    for what he is – my friend.

Martin's Poem

It isn't easy
   trying to describe
      someone special.
Not that words
   aren't available;
but the thoughts
just don't come.
It might be easier
   to say,
"Friend, I like you."

A friend he is
   in his special way.
He doesn't say much,
   but seems glad
      friends are near.
Then, ten-year-olds
   don't express their feelings.

He's very special,
   full of life, happy,
   good natured, loving.
Anyone who meets this
   handsome, blonde haired,
      blue-eyed lad

would easily take to his
    charm.
Words written,
saying nothing much.
Just a few thoughts
    dedicated to a
fascinating young man.
Another friend – Martin.

Steele

Young man,
Observed from a distance,
touched from afar.

Friendship knows no age limits.
My best is brought out
   when in his presence.
Hope is kindled where
   once only ashes lay.

Joy comes from giving
   And living and loving.
If I am an example,
   someone to be admired
      and seen as a good role model
Then all is right –
   everything is possible,
      There is no boundary.

Young man,
observed from a distance,
touched from afar.

My friend, for whom
   I give my all.

Haley

Boy.
Paths cross, at random
    or in destiny.
Can fate just be a simple
    toss of the coin?
Is it true that acquaintances
    happen so?

The knowing has just been
    fairly recent,
but it seems as though
    comradeship has been eternal.
Can such things be?

Trails cross, diverge,
    and cross again.
Such is the chance of calculated
    fate.
Our trails are now at
    the crossroads.
I am proud, joy fills my heart.
    Boy and friend.

Star

Have you ever met a movie star?
I did once in Cokeville.
We didn't speak or shake hands
    that Sunday.
I just stared –
    he glanced my way.
He was only a thirteen-year-old.
So what could I say?

I wondered if he thought
    I had recognized him.
I'll admit it wasn't easy --
    the recognition.
That day he was wearing glasses.
He didn't before.
Everything else was the same:
hair, eyes, face, actions, all --
    the same.

I wondered if our paths might cross
again even if in some distant year.
Would we speak then, or remain silent?
And would we become friends,
or remain strangers?

These were my thoughts
when I met the star.

Hope

What have we if not children?
   Nothing.
I cannot imagine
   the world without a child's
     laughter and games.
It would be so sad,
   so pathetic ––
a world without children.
   Dreary, dismal.
Adults don't get along well:
children are beautiful.
   Little people,
all full of love of life
   and a deep-rooted faith
     in the world,
an innocence,
that's really startling.
Where is the faith of the adult?
   Dead.

So, where is our hope?
   In the children
     if only we believe,
for the little ones are a
   promise of the future

and a great blessing
for the present
if they aren't spoiled,
desecrated
by the monsters of the world.

We the adults,
we the monsters,
have hope.

Human Boy

Behold a human boy
   and marvel
at his works.
All that he does
   whether ornery
   or good
seems to be a God-send;
it is just his nature.
He may be upsetting
   and a puzzle
   at times
but he is an angel
   none-the-less.
Oh, glorious to be
   a human
     boy!

Twice Told

The boy smiles.
The boy shrugs.
It seems he's done this
    once before.
Pinching apples from
    Old Mr. Barnes
    is really stealing.
"There's no room in society
    for a thief," Barnes says.

Maybe thieves are important.
They keep everyone else
    on their toes.

The boy smiles.
The boy shrugs.
He's certainly done this
    once before.

Little Blue Boy

I saw him sitting there
   beaten by circumstances;
lonely, neglected, unwanted,
   unloved.
He had haunting
   big blue eyes
which could pierce a humane heart.
So sad,
he only wanted someone
   to notice, to care.
But there he sat in society's prison --
the coldest of institutions.

He will someday learn
   to strike back
   at the system
     which killed his spirit.
And he will lay his life down,
for our errors.
Reach out to him,
   if you possess any goodness,
   before it's too late
     and he becomes
     an angry young man.

The Boy

A boy is a fascinating,
    marvelous, beautiful creature.
He runs and jumps and climbs;
actions which are just natural
for him to do.
After all,
    he is a boy;
a boy who possesses love
    of life and knowledge
that there's always a new
adventure around each corner.
His games bespeak a desire
to be grown up.
That, too, is a boy.
The boy is impish in a way
    which becomes him.
And this is sure.
The boy, the young man,
lives with a sense of
    adventurous life.

I Often Wonder

I often wonder what to say
To the little boy I watch at play.
He has such a charming way
In all his actions from day to day.

I realize he's just a little man
Accomplishing feats in God's great plan.
And he always exclaimed, "Yes I can'"
He turned his head, and away he ran.

Little Child

Little child,
   love is in your heart,
      joy is in your soul.
My laughter comes
   when I behold
what you have, what you are,
   in your simple
      innocence and faith.
Your spirit is free
   and soars to mystical
kingdoms and palaces
   of untold imaginations.

My heart cries with joy
   when I behold the
      rapture and sunshine
on your face when you
   see sights and life's magic
      unfurling before
   your eyes so bright and shining.

Oh, that such peace as is
   yours will remain
      from spring to summer,
   from fall to winter.

Your gold should be pure
    and remain bright as
diamonds now and forever.

Little child!
    Little child!
I seek your peace and joy
    and desire to share
my dreams and schemes,
    my ideals and plans --
        my life -- with you.
You are my child, my hope,
    my dreams come true.

Ah, Little Man

Ah, little man, my own,
   what dreams and hopes
are locked in your mind?
I see the twinkle
   in your eye
and the upturned lips,
     and I know
   there is some deviltry afoot.

Ah, little one, my own,
   what dares and cares
furrow you brow?
I want to share your joy
   and laughter,
your yearning and learning,
   your hopes and fears,
     sorrow and tears.

But my little one, my own,
   our roads are not the same.
We traverse different lanes.
My trail goes on before.
Although I lead,
   you may not follow.
That is our course of life.

You are me and I am you,
    but we are different entities.
I cannot share your future.
And if I were to try,
    I would, I must fail.
This is the rule of generations.

Ah, my little one, my own,
    my son, my son,
        Little man.

Sidewalk Surfer

I saw him first
on a skateboard.
I thought he was mad
   racing around trying
   oh so very hard to break his neck.
Why, the lad must have
been doing at least ninety,
   or so I thought,
as his hair was streaming
behind him.
Surely he had scars from
   past speed record runs.
Anyone going that fast on
a skateboard who happened
   by some chance of fate
   to hit a rock or crack
      was sure to dismember himself!

But he rode on as though
he had not a care or worry
   in the world.
Nerves of steel he had, no doubt.
But not I,
   my mother never raised
      a bloody fool.

I suppose we all have our fancies:
to each his own.
The lad sought heaven
on a skate board.
   And I?
      I sought heaven in poetry.

Blank Page

A blank page is a fascinating
thing to behold.
With it a person can do
    marvelous things.
A term paper is expressed,
a novel born.
And all started with
    a blank page.

Children are also
    blank pages.
Lives can be patterned
and created like
    stories and novels.
The type is set at birth,
the chapters are written
    while growth occurs.
Those persons who surround
    the keys
are the authors of
the finished 'story'.

Let us beware
    lest the completed story
    is rejected by the
    publisher.

Daydream

In his mind he is the
 star pitcher, or perhaps
the greatest first baseman in
 the history of baseball.

I wonder what he sees as I
 behold him sitting there
 with his head resting on
  his arms,
the fielder's mitt on his hand.
What wonders do those bright
 blue eyes behold as he
 stares into his future?
What dreams may come
 to that head covered by
 unkempt blonde hair?

He sits as if all the world
revolves around him and his
 quiet thoughts.
For him all the world is a
 wondrous stage, a
 panorama of hopes and
  ideals.

I will not, I must not,
   deny him his dreams,
   or curb his hopes and
earnestly sought for wishes.
   I will not touch his ambitions.
   After all I am but an adult,
     one whose dreams are in
     the past.

May you always have daydreams,
   my little one, my son.
     And make your dreams
     come true.

A Better Way

I saw a little child laughing
and wondered what special
secrets lay locked inside
that beautiful head.
He seemed to be enjoying
Himself so much, visions
of candied delights must
have overwhelmed his being.
Perhaps thoughts of marvelous
toys played upon him.

Oh, it must be grand
to be a child with all
his dreams and games and joys!
And all is innocence
where little ones are concerned.

What a shame their laughter
and their loveliness must be
spoiled by their growing old.
So sad is the course of events,

and so long the road of maturity
that we lose what we once were.
We cannot look back,
But must always press forward.
Our only joy is in children's laughter.
It is for the sake of the children
that we adults must find a better way.

And A Little Child Shall Lead Them

O, but it's good
   to be alive!

Life is like the world
   in summer.
Everything is young
   and fresh and vibrant.
The fields are ripe,
   ready for the harvest.

Someday,
after all the wars
   have been fought,
a small child
shall lead us to the harvest.
As long as there are children
   there is hope
and a promise of better things.
For in the little people
   lies salvation
   for man.
No sword and no lance
shall destroy them;
no word shall corrupt them.

The small ones are free;
Their freedom shall free us,
for so it has been written.
And a little child
   shall lead them.

Seasons

Seasons

I often think of life
as a year -- composed of seasons.
We grow and live and age
   and then die.
Thus the cycle of life.
It is proper, a necessity
   for our purpose
     and the purpose
       of One who sent us.

I

Spring.
Flowers sprout and bloom,
buds appear and open on greenery,
grass climbs toward the sky;
birds nest, hatch eggs, and sing.
A new cycle of life beginning.

So it is with man.
We are born, we learn,
   we experience, we grow.

Childhood.
A time of experience and wonders.
Our spring.

II

Summer
All is as it should be.
Everything is grown and full of life.
Plants and animals are in their prime.
All is well.

Man, too, has his summer.
We find love, marry, raise children.
We work and play and laugh.
All our dreams from spring seem real.
Life unfolds with each new experience.
All is fulfilled.

III

Autumn.
Things lose their shades of brightness.
Aging sets in.
Where once green, brown.
Warm breezes give way to chills.
And all is well.

So, too, man has autumn.

Our lives change.
We notice lines and a touch of gray.
Our steps become slower, less certain.
Appetites wane.
We become grumpy
   and less tolerant of youth.
Life becomes dull.
The cycle continues.

IV

Winter.
Nature seems bleak,
   the air, crisp and cold.
Snow blankets the earth
where once flowers bloomed,
and icicles hang in trees
   replacing leaves.

Winter for man comes.
We hobble around with canes.
Things seem blurred to view
   and hearing-aids are necessary.
Sleep comes.
The cycle completed.

And with sleep comes
   A new awakening,
     A new beginning.
Nothing ever ends.

All is well ...
   All is well.

Autumn

Autumn.
A time of change, a time of passage.
   The days become cool
   and the nights chill.
Darkness descends more
   quickly each day.
Leaves turn and become,
instead of green, shades
   of crimson, gold,
     and brown.

Autumn.
The time of holidays and
   sacred events.
   For this is the time
of Halloween, when ghosts
   and goblins and beasties
appear with the shout, "Trick or treat!"
It is the season when friends
   and family gather for
     the joy and pleasantness
of Thanksgiving; still at Grandma's.

Autumn.
The time of ending, and preparation
   for rebirth.
For with the end of autumn
   and beginning of winter comes
      the advent of the most
glorious time of year.
   The time of hope, and
   promise, and joy,
      and peace –
   Christmas

Christmas I

I love the sound of Christmas bells
    and singing carolers on the street.
And my heart is warmed by
    the laughter and greetings of
        folks one chances to meet.

It is a special time when
    hearts are glad and joy is shared.
And more than the gift received
    is the gift given out of love.

Christmas is special.
Of all the seasons to be celebrated
    and shared throughout the lands,
        the celebration of the birth
            of Christ is best.
So, let us not forget the greatest gift --
    Christmas!

Christmas II

Once again it's the time of year
    to think of friends both far and near.
And by remembering those good times past.
    they will not fade, but must always last.
Therefore, with this verse, goes a part of me
    to touch that spirit which dwells in thee.

Something's In the Air

There's something in the air.
People are unusually friendly
   and smiles are everywhere.
Pass someone on the street
   and you sense the greeting
      though it wasn't said.

The nod and the twinkle in an eye
   are vibrant.
Something's in the air
   It's Christmas!

Christmas Message

Hearts are broken tonight
and everywhere there is fright.
But God has seen our sorrows
and mended our tomorrows,
for on this night the angels sing
"Christ is born to earth as King!"

Yuletide thought

It's great to know
    that the time has come again
to get out the wrapping paper,
    the ribbon and tape,
tinsel, decorations for the tree.
Only once a year does
    this day come.
Let's be happy and merry.
    It's Christmas.

Tinsel Season

It seems a joyous season --
Christmas with all its
    glitter and excitement.
Not that other seasons
aren't joyous, they are.
But Christmas has a touch
    Of magic about it.
All through December
trees are decorated and
    lights hung for show,
turkeys and all kinds of
    fabulous foodstuffs bought,
and scores of presents picked
    out and wrapped.
All the hustle and bustle
just for that special morn
    when it's off to Grandma's
    or Uncle Pete's or Aunt Clara's
        to exchange gifts
        and share love with family, friends.
Yes,
    Christmas is a most joyous
        and magical season,
for expressed and greatly stressed
    is care and love.

A Christmas Thought

The world once lay
in darkness and sin.
Hope seemed distant, removed.
And the righteous cried
    unto heaven:
        persecution was great.

But miracle above all miracles,
God heard the cries and prayers
and sent His Son to dwell
    upon the earth
        for a season,
that man might yet be redeemed,
    forgiven, brought back to
        celestial glory.

That first Christmas proved
God loved His Children
and had not forgotten them.
Thus lay the hope of
    peace on earth
        goodwill toward men.

Year's End Message

As the fading year ends,
It's good to think of friends,
And marvel at fortune good
With all the blessings one should.

With the start of another year
It's great to spread good cheer.
And with our friends a special blessing
One marked with greatest stressing.

So I say to you, my friends,
Until all eternity ends,
Merry Christmas and Happy New Year,
for I hold your friendship dear.

Blanket of Snow

Often have I seen
the glitter and sparkle
of the chilly and unusual blanket,
and paused to wonder and reflect.

Pity that person who has never
known thee, O Blanket!
Your diamond luster blinds
when open to the sun
and glimmers like priceless jewels
when beheld by the moon.

Wonder of wonders is the
reigning queen of precious beauty
which never utter a single command,
but is majestic none-the-less.

Behold the Empress,
Blanket of Snow!

Snow

I saw something white fall from the sky today.
It was such an odd thing.
It came floating down as if it were but a feather.
As it landed on the ground or in my hand
   when I reached out for it,
      it melted and turned into water.
For a long time this substance from the heavens
fell, landed, and melted. But eventually
the substance ceased to melt as it landed,
but rather collected, thus covering the ground
with a white beauty that only poets think about.
A substance called snow.

Season

Flowers bloom in the spring
and workings uncounted
seem to tell a story of destiny.
A gentle breeze stirs
and brings life to all
the marvels which grow.
This is life.

February

February can be bleak.
Depressing might be the
    word to use --
each has his own thought.
Melancholy, too, is a
    word to express
the feelings of the cold
wind,
    relentlessly blowing
    from the north.
It seems that spring,
    with all her charm and beauty,
        will never come.
Although it's cold and
    dismal -- February --
the sky is often clear and blue.
This is a certain reassurance
    that all is not lost.
Spring will come.
February will never last
    forever.

This Valentine's Day

Of course again it's time for valentines.
It happens once a year.
   And as the fleeting years roll by
       acquaintances are brought to mind.
With the memory, a sense of loss,
   for in our daily living
       we oft times forget the
       caring and sharing
   of friends and those we hold
          so dear.
And moments lost are never gained.
   We lose the experience of watching
   and living with the ones
       around us.
For the moments lost –- the shadows in time –-
   I must repent.
       I must learn to give,
       and care, and share.

With this new beginning
   and understanding
I must say today,
   This valentine's Day,
      Be my valentine,
         be my friend.

Nature's Truth

There is a truth
   in nature.
Though it's overlooked
   by most,
it lies there all the
   same.
Trees, shrubs, flowers,
   the grass of spring;
all springing to life
   as though
there had been no
   winter.
If man had thought
them dead in the autumn
he was mistaken.
The old just stepped
   aside
for the new.
And, thus, the secret.
It's nothing new,
   just a wise fact —
nothing dies,
   it's only
replaced.

War

War

I hear drums and bugles
   once again.
With them comes the sound
   of marching feet and
     singing men.

   The war was on!

Over countless battlefields
armies come, fight,
   kill, die.
Cries run through the night;
   cries of maimed
     men, boys.
For this they are born, live:
   to suffer and sweat and bleed.

   Why?
     The war is on!

Tomorrow brings the dream
   of peace.
All is well.
   A new generation of boys
   is born to play with
     toy guns in
     pretend wars.

The old men, politicians,
wait and plan and create
   situations.
Glory is dreamed
   for young men.

And again the cry,
   "The war is on!"

The creators of war
   cannot understand.
They see no battlefields.
   They're safe to cry,
     "The war is on!"

We never learn the truth.
It knows no understanding.
Hate and greed annoy,
   passions mount,
   blood-lust reigns
     to claim a truly
     lost generation –
      the dead!

Yes,
   I see flames of conflict
raging helter-skelter
   around our pitiful
   existence.
No end can come when
   the war is on …
     is on …
       on …

Vietnamese Boy

I see you before me
  when I wake in
    the morning.
I see you before me
  when I go to bed.
You are always with me.

I behold your eight or nine
  year old lifeless body
    being loaded into an
  Army ambulance.
I see the puddle of blood
  in the road where
  you lay after the
    speeding jeep ran over you.
I see your mother and
  grandmother getting into the
    ambulance and hear their
      wailing of grief.

I feel guilt by being part of the
  army that killed you.
    Forgive me!

You would be middle-aged now
    with children and grandchildren.
I mourn your loss still and all
    of the truly lost generations.

    Vietnamese boy, lost
        but never forgotten.

A Boy Speaking of His Dream

Let me tell you about my dream –
the one I have had several times.

Look here.
I am a soldier lying in a fox hole.
I have been rendered helpless by wounds
and am without the means of defending myself.
I see enemy soldiers advancing
across the grassless plain.
I recognize the gleam of metal shining in the sun
as enemy bayonets.
I know that I am going to die.
All I can do is watch the enemy come
closer, closer … closer.

Behold.
The enemy are standing over me
with their teeth clenched in hate.
Terror grips me as they raise their bayonets.
They thrust them into my body again and again.
I feel sharp pain … and then numbness … as my body
twitches in an effort to stave off death.
I am enclosed in darkness … and then nothingness …
Death.

Heroes

I wonder why the trend today
is to slander our heroes.
They were great men of courage,
   not the killers some would
      have us believe.
There is pain in the lies,
an agony that cannot be ended.
   Half-truths cannot be the fact.
      The records speak for themselves.
The heroes remain heroes,
never to be diminished or tarnished
   by the bigotry and slander
      of the few who bear false witness.

Yes.
   The records speak for themselves.
     The famous remain golden
     and pure.
They were and are and ever shall be ...
       heroes.

May God Have Mercy

So the war has come.
And you have gone
    to kill and maim.
May God have mercy.

You, who march
    to preserve
a false way of life,
who march for
    corrupt political
        ideals,
and who have been
    misled
by the clamor
    of the uninformed,
are doomed.

War is
    and leads to
        hell.

So unto all nations —
may God have mercy.

Friend …

You talk of enlisting
in the Army.
I don't want you to go.
I fear for you.
But why should I?
You're no kin of mine,
though I wish you were.
It's just that I wish you well.
Friend, I love you.

My Dead Friend

Alas, my friend is dead!
He lived and loved, and is now no more.
Such is the burden of life.
Great is the loss, much is the sting,
but I must accept it and live.

Can That Be True?

Can't you see the little boys,
One with all the fancy toys?
It's all for one, and one for all.
Just climb on o'er MacMurray's wall;
Never ask the reason why,
Been granted courage to do or die.
Running and jumping,
Jostling and tossing,
Hiking and biking,
Coming and going,
Romping and playing, all.
Ever ready for that sudden fall.
Cowboys and Indians, and army, too.
Having a ball if that be true.
Can that be true?
Can that be true?

Can't you see the little girls,
With pony tails and oodles of curls?
It's here today and gone tomorrow,
With little time to go and borrow.
Pretty dolls and pretty houses,
Pretty skirts and pretty blouses.
Sewing and mending,
Cooking and blending,

Singing and humming,
Going and coming,
Shopping and washing, all.
Ever ready for that sudden fall.
Dreaming and hoping, and planning, too.
Having a ball if that be true.
Can that be true?
Can that be true?

Observers

I

There is not reason on this earth.
Only madness, blindness.

Man is not free,
but rather a slave of his
ambitions, greed's, lusts,
    and prejudices.
We are prejudiced because that is what
    the rules of life dictate.
These rules, which are passed
    from one generation to the next,
are received and carried out
    without question.
We do not think, we only act.
We forget, or do not heed,
    our religions which teach
brotherhood, love, and trust
    among all peoples.

"Do unto others before
    they do unto you,"
is the 'Golden Rule' of the day.
We despise all good,
    and desire all evil.

We can ask any man we meet
    on the street
why he attends church regularly
and he will answer,
    "Prestige.
        There is no God,
        only prestige."
(This must be today's magic word.)

Who's to say that these things
    are true?
Who's to say that they are false?
After all, we are only observers.

II

There is not reason on this earth.
Only madness, blindness.

All nations scream,
    "We want peace!!!
        We want peace!!!
            We want peace!!!"
A piece of what?
War? Territory? Prestige
    as a world power? Popularity?
Perhaps we are not satisfied
with ourselves, our present
    state of affairs.
We must have everything,
    or nothing.
Our slogans are 'Win or lose',
    'Kill or be killed',
        'Eat or be eaten'.
Therefore, we wage war
against our neighbors.

And what care our politicians?
They're not the ones who have to
    fight and die for the
        'Great Cause'.
No.
The politicians only start the wars
    which the boys must finish.
"If ten thousand boys are killed,"
    say the politicians,
"We can send in ten thousand more."
The nations may cry, "Peace,"
but in reality,
    there is no peace.
We have failed ourselves,
    our children, and
        our grandchildren,
and we know it.
We cannot make corrections
    where they cannot be made
History repeats itself.
And so we go on living;
    doing what we did before.
we never ask ourselves why
    we do the same things
        over and over again
probably because we are
afraid of the alternate paths:
    the much safer, saner paths.
But should this be so?
Who's to say that they are false?
After all, we are only observers.

Observers only observe,
    nothing more …